T0149496

Jesus Loves Me

A Follow-Up Guide for Children

Keith D. Pisani

WESTBOW
PRESS®
A DIVISION OF THOMAS NELSON
& ZONDERVAN

Copyright © 2017 Keith D. Pisani.

All rights reserved. No part of this book may be used or reproduced by any means, graphic, electronic, or mechanical, including photocopying, recording, taping or by any information storage retrieval system without the written permission of the author except in the case of brief quotations embodied in critical articles and reviews.

Scripture taken from the King James Version of the Bible

This book is a work of non-fiction. Unless otherwise noted, the author and the publisher make no explicit guarantees as to the accuracy of the information contained in this book and in some cases, names of people and places have been altered to protect their privacy.

WestBow Press books may be ordered through booksellers or by contacting:

WestBow Press
A Division of Thomas Nelson & Zondervan
1663 Liberty Drive
Bloomington, IN 47403
www.westbowpress.com
1 (866) 928-1240

Because of the dynamic nature of the Internet, any web addresses or links contained in this book may have changed since publication and may no longer be valid. The views expressed in this work are solely those of the author and do not necessarily reflect the views of the publisher, and the publisher hereby disclaims any responsibility for them.

Any people depicted in stock imagery provided by Thinkstock are models, and such images are being used for illustrative purposes only. Certain stock imagery © Thinkstock.

ISBN: 978-1-5127-7061-2 (sc)
ISBN: 978-1-5127-7060-5 (e)

Library of Congress Control Number: 2016921545

Print information available on the last page.

WestBow Press rev. date: 11/13/2019

Introduction

Perhaps the most recognizable children's song of all time is the following.

Jesus loves me— This I know,
For the Bible tells me so;
Little ones to Him belong—
They are weak, but He is strong.

Refrain:

Yes, Jesus loves me!
Yes, Jesus loves me!
Yes, Jesus loves me!
The Bible tells me so.[1]

Based on the words of this time-honored song, my wife and I have developed a follow-up guide for children who

---

[1] "Jesus Loves Me" is a popular hymn written in 1860 by Anna B. Warner (William B. Bradbury added the music in 1862). "Jesus Loves Me," *Wikipedia: The Free Encyclopedia* (July 26, 2015). Wikimedia Foundation, Inc. Retrieved January 6, 2016, from http://www.wikipedia.org.

have recently received Jesus Christ as Savior. Most follow-up studies are designed for use with adults. Since Jesus said, "Let the little children come to Me, and do not forbid them; for of such is the kingdom of heaven" (Matthew 19:14), we sensed the importance of producing a follow-up guide that children can understand.

Children need discipled just as much as any other age group. They are the future of the church. By using this follow-up guide for children, you are helping the next generation grow in the grace and knowledge of our Lord and Savior Jesus Christ (2 Peter 3:18).

May God bless the lives of all who study God's Word for the purpose of growth. My prayer is that all who participate in this Jesus Loves Me study will practice the "Word-centered" life. Enjoy your time in God's Word.[2]

---

[2] All scripture references are from the 1611 King James Version of the Bible.

Training Notes for the Discipler

Just as physical babies should not be left on the doorstep to fend for themselves, neither should spiritual babies be left to grow on their own. Paul's approach to discipleship was "as a nurse cherisheth her children: so being affectionately desirous of you, we were willing to have imparted unto you, not the gospel of God only, but also our own souls, because ye were dear to us" (1 Thessalonians 1:6–7). The early church cared for new converts as a mother cares for her newborn. Should the modern church do less?

Follow-up is the initial phase of discipleship. It begins after a person receives Jesus Christ as Savior. The salvation experience may take place inside the church at an altar call, in a classroom, through a children's ministry, or during a harvest event. A person may come to Christ and experience regeneration outside the church during an outreach event, one-on-one or group evangelism, with a believer, or in the privacy of a person's one-on-One time with God. Wherever salvation happens, Christians are responsible to initiate follow-up. The purpose of follow-up is spiritual growth toward maturity in Jesus Christ.

Physical babies grow. Babies who do not grow are given special medical attention to promote physical growth. Just as a non growing physical baby is considered an aberration, it is considered "not normal" for a babe in Christ to remain spiritually immature. Just as first-century believers grew, "in the grace and knowledge of our Lord and Savior Jesus Christ" (2 Peter 3:18), modern believers should grow into maturity for Jesus Christ.

When a person receives Jesus Christ as Savior, a believer trained in the four Jesus Loves Me follow-up sessions should copy the first session and give one copy to the new convert, keeping one copy for himself or herself. The believer, now called the "discipler," will take the new convert, open the first session, and review the instructions on the top of the first study. "My name is _____" is the name of the new convert being discipled. "My helper's name and phone number (contact information) are _____" is the name of the discipler. Both the new convert and the discipler need a Bible for study and a writing instrument (a pen or pencil) to fill in the blanks and take notes.

The four sessions are keyed to the 1611 King James Version of the Bible and include the reading content of instructive opening paragraphs, fill-in-the-blank questions, matching, some memorization, and some writing. The minimal qualifications needed to use the follow-up materials as a discipler are that he or she is a believer and able to read.

If both the discipler and the new convert are available, the first session can begin immediately, or at a prescribed time in an approved setting. Males disciple males and females, females. Only approved workers should follow-up children. When children are involved, their parents or guardians should give approval before follow-up begins.

The sessions are taught, or led, out loud by the discipler. Christ said in Matthew 28:18–19, that "teaching" is an effective discipleship method. Also, at the end of session 1, the discipler and new convert can, with approval of the parent or guardian, arrange for a prescribed place, date, and time to meet for session 2. After session 2 is completed, the discipler and new convert can establish a prescribed place, date, and time to meet for session 3. The same pattern is followed for session 4.

After the new convert's salvation experience, if the discipler and the new convert have a scheduling conflict and cannot begin immediately, the discipler should make an appointment with the new convert and establish a prescribed place, date, and time when both can meet. If no time is available, the discipler can assign the first study as a take-home assignment to be brought back for review with the discipler at a prescribed place, date, and time. If this latter arrangement is made, the discipler will review the answers to session 1, make comments, and then teach or lead session 2 to the new convert. At the conclusion of session 2, the discipler can follow the same procedure for the remaining assignments. Once all four sessions have been completed, the new convert should ask the church's pastor about baptism and church membership.

In making disciples, it is important to remember we are not making disciples of ourselves. We are making disciples of Jesus Christ. It is a privilege to serve Jesus in making disciples of new converts and seeing them grow into maturity for Christ. May God bless the use of these follow-up studies. My prayer is that all believers will grow into maturity for Christ.[3]

_____

[3] Parts of the Jesus Loves Me study are keyed to the adult versions of this study by Keith D. Pisani, the four-session *Spiritual Lessons for New Believers* follow-up book, the twenty-six session content book *Spiritual Lessons for Growing Believers*, and the companion workbook, *Spiritual Lessons for Growing Believers Workbook*. All can be obtained through WestBow Press or through the author's personal website, www.keithpisaniministries.com.

Follow-Up 1: Jesus Loves Me

My name is _____.

My helper's name and phone number are _____

_____.

Please read the following paragraph aloud.

Most people like to be loved. Do you? Sometimes the people around us love us for who we are as a family member or friend, or for what we can do for them, such as chores at home or work at school. Jesus loves us without conditions. As God, Jesus loves us because of who *He* is. His greatest act of love took place at Calvary, where He died on a cross for your sins. Jesus loves you. Jesus died for you. He lives in heaven today because He wants you to experience His grace and His love.

The purpose of this study is to share some truths about the salvation from sin that Jesus provides for you. Read the scripture references given. Then write your answers in the spaces provided.

1. Why do we need salvation; why did Jesus have to die for our sins?

In the book God wrote—His Word, the Bible—He said that we are sinners. We do wrong things. Sometimes we think bad thoughts, go to places we should not go, or not do good things that we should do. All of this is sin. What did God say about sin in His Word? Fill in the blanks.

_____ have sinned and come short of the "entry requirements" to get in to God's heaven. (Romans 3:23)

"All" means "all," and that's all that all can mean. I have sinned. You have sinned. Everyone has sinned, except Jesus (2 Corinthians 5:21; 1 Peter 2:22). Because Jesus Christ is God and never sinned, He is the only one who can please God's standard of holiness and right living. He is the only one who meets the entry requirements to get into God's heaven. For us to get into heaven, we must enter with Jesus. When we enter with Jesus, God will not look at you, the sinner, and say no. Instead, He will look at Jesus *in* you and, based on the holiness of Jesus Christ, God will say yes to you and let you into His heaven.

Jesus said, "I am the _____, the _____, and the _____, no one comes to the Father (gets into God's heaven) except through Him." (John 14:6)

Who owns the house in which you live? Your dad? Your mom? Your parents? Your grandmother? Your guardian? Whoever owns your house has the right to say who can or cannot come in. Who owns heaven? God owns heaven. Because God owns heaven, He established the entry requirement for getting into His heaven as having a personal relationship with Jesus Christ through salvation (John 14:6). God lets you into His heaven because of Jesus.

2. What is it about sin (doing, thinking, or saying wrong things) that keeps us out of heaven?

Have you ever said something to someone and he or she did not like it? Have you ever offended someone? When we sin, we offend God. When we offend God, we deserve punishment. The punishment we deserve for offending God is an eternity—forever—spent in a very bad place called hell (the lake of fire). It is the place where the devil lives. It is where people go who do not have a personal relationship with Jesus Christ as Savior. How do we know that sinners deserve eternal punishment? Fill in the blanks.

The _____ of sin is death. (Romans 6:23a)

"Wages" are things we earn. In the Bible, the word "death" means "separation." When we die physically, our souls are separated from our physical bodies. The soul lives forever. If we know Jesus Christ as Savior, the soul will live forever in heaven. If we do not know Jesus Christ as Savior, the soul will live forever in hell where we will experience 'spiritual' death (separation from God forever). Would you rather go to heaven and live forever with the God who loves you enough to provide a way for you to go to heaven? Or would you rather be separated from the God of love forever and go to the bad place, which is a lake that burns with fire (hell)?

_____ Heaven _____ Hell

For God demonstrated His _____ toward us, in that, while we were yet sinners, Christ died for us. (Romans 5:8)

As sinners, we have done too many bad things for a holy God to let us into His heaven, and we have not done enough good things for a holy God to let us into His heaven. Since sinners do not deserve to go to heaven based on our own merits (good actions), how did God work it out that sinners can enter His heaven? In spite of our sins, God loved us. God's holiness requires a punishment for our sins. But because Jesus Christ experienced our punishment for us at Calvary, God's love lets us into His heaven when we have Jesus Christ as our Savior.

3. What must a sinner do to be saved (to be "saved" means to have a personal relationship with Jesus)?

Salvation does not just happen. Although God provides the salvation, sinners have a responsibility to act on what He provides. We have a responsibility to ask Jesus into our lives as our personal Lord and Savior.

But as many as _____ Him (Jesus), to
      them God gives the power (ability) to become

the sons (children) of God, to as many as believe on His name. (John 1:12).

The term "receive" means to "warmly welcome" and speaks of an invitation to enter a home.

Has someone you have not seen for a while ever come to visit? When that person comes, are you so happy to see the visitor you jump for joy, hug the person, and invite him or her into your house? Your life, your heart, is like a house. God wants your heart to be His home. For your heart to be God's home, you must invite Him into your life as your personal Lord and Savior.

If you have not invited Christ into your life as your Lord and Savior, take the time to do it now. How do you ask Jesus into your life?

Admit that you are a sinner (Romans 3:10, 23).

Acknowledge that sin deserves eternal punishment (Romans 6:23a).

Recognize that, on the cross at Calvary, Jesus Christ experienced your punishment for you (Romans 5:8).

Ask Jesus into your life as your personal Lord and Savior (John 1:12; Romans 10:9–10).

God said, "That if you confess with your mouth the Lord Jesus and believe in your heart that God has raised Him from the dead, you will be saved. For with the heart one believes unto righteousness, and with the mouth confession is made unto salvation" (Romans 10:9–10). The term "confess" means you agree with God that you are a sinner. To "believe" means that, by faith, you trust Jesus to get you into God's heaven. Because you, "confess with your mouth," that Jesus Christ is God (Lord, Master, and Savior of your life), there is a point in time when you experience salvation and are saved. If today is the day when you used your words to ask Jesus into your life and believed in your heart that He saved you, write the date in the space provided.

I received Jesus Christ as my personal Lord and Savior on this date: _____, _____.

If you have never received Jesus into your life as Savior, pray this prayer now aloud in front of your helper. You pray this prayer in front of your helper so he or she knows that you understand what you must do to be saved.

Dear Lord, I am a sinner. I have done wrong things. I deserve eternal punishment. Jesus Christ experienced my punishment for me at Calvary. I apply what Jesus did on the cross to my life. I ask Jesus into my life as my personal Lord and Savior. Thank You, God, for saving my soul and forgiving my sins. Thank You that I will go to heaven. In Jesus's name I pray, Amen!

If you meant that prayer sincerely, then you are saved. Your sins are forgiven. You will go to heaven when you die because Jesus is in your life as your Savior.

Response Notes:

4. For your personal study, look up the following Bible verses.

I am a sinner.	Romans 3:10, 23; Isaiah 64:6
Sin deserves eternal punishment.	Romans 5:12; John 3:18; Ezekiel 18:4c
Jesus Christ experienced the sinner's punishment for us.	Romans 5:6, 8; John 3:16; 1 Peter 2:24
To go to heaven, sinners must ask Jesus into their live as their personal Lord and Savior	Romans 10:9–10; John 1:12; 14:6; 1 Peter 1:18–19; Ephesians 2:8–9; Acts 4:12; Titus 3:5

Are you sure you are saved?
_____ Yes _____ Not Sure. If not sure, make sure today.

Follow-Up 2: This I Know

My name is _____.

My helper's name and phone number are _____

_____.

Please read the following paragraph aloud.

When a sinner receives Jesus Christ into his or her life as Savior, the individual experiences forgiveness of sins and is promised a home in heaven. The person is a new creation in Jesus Christ (2 Corinthians 5:17). He or she is saved. He or she is a Christian ("Christ-one"). The person is a believer in Jesus Christ. Though saved, the sinner may doubt his or her salvation. If this happens to you, the God who owns heaven, the God who has promised to let you into His heaven, has given us some scripture verses that tell us we can be sure we are saved. This is called "assurance of salvation."

Has there ever been a time in your life when people said something that sounded true, but you did not know whether you should trust their word as true? Did you ever doubt something that someone has said? It is one thing to doubt a person's word, but it is another thing to doubt God's Word. The God who owns heaven gives His Word that once you are saved, you will never lose that salvation.

The purpose of this study is to share some truths about the assurance of your salvation, that once saved, always saved. Read the scripture references given. Then write your answers in the spaces provided.

1. How long does salvation last?

    The person who believes in Jesus Christ knows he or she has _____ _____ (1 John 5:13).

    The person who has eternal life shall never _____ (John 10:28).

    The word "perish" means to go to the "bad place" (hell).

2. Who guarantees that salvation will last forever?

    The _____ Himself bears witness with our spirit that we are the _____ of God (Romans 8:16).

The "Spirit" in Romans 8:16 is God's Holy Spirit, who "takes up residence in us" (He lives in us) once we are saved. He can live in us because He does not have a physical body; He is a spirit. We do not see air, yet just as air fills your lungs, God's Holy Spirit can live in your body and life even though God's Holy Spirit, like air, is invisible.

The believer is kept (guaranteed salvation) by the power of _____ through faith unto salvation (1 Peter 1:5).

We do not keep ourselves saved by good deeds or by any other way. The God who saved us keeps us saved.

3. Read 1 John 5:12. Then answer the following question.

Are you sure that you will enter heaven beyond this life?
_____ Yes _____ Not Sure

You get the Son when you ask Jesus into your life as Savior. If you have God's Son living in your life, the God who owns heaven says that you are saved. If you never asked Jesus into your life as personal Lord and Savior, then you are not saved.

Do you have God's Son in your life as your personal Lord and Savior? Did you ask Jesus into your life? If so, you are saved, and God promises that you will go to heaven.

4. Based on your understanding of the Bible, answer the following question.

If you were to die today and meet God, and He should ask you why He should let you into His heaven, what would you say?

_____

_____

_____

_____

_____

_____

If you say anything other than, "I asked Jesus into my life as my Savior," you need to review your salvation experience and make sure that you have asked Jesus into your life (see "Follow-Up 1 on how to be saved). If you are ever in doubt as to whether you are saved, it is never a problem to repeat your request for salvation prayer to God until you are sure that you are saved. Remember, if you have Jesus in your life as your personal Lord and Savior, God's Word promises you salvation (Romans 10:13). If you have Jesus in your life, you are saved and do not need to get saved again. God says, "Once saved, always saved." You are eternally secure in Jesus.

5. John 3:16 describes how God provided for humankind's salvation. Make this verse personal. Please place your name in the spaces provided.

   For God so loved _____, that He gave His only (uniquely) begotten Son (Jesus); that _____ who believes in Him should not perish but that _____ should have everlasting life (John 3:16).

6. Review sections 1 through 5. Answer the following questions.

   Have you received Jesus Christ as your personal Lord and Savior? _____ Yes _____ No

   Are your sins forgiven? _____ Yes _____ No

How do you know that you have everlasting—eternal—life?

_____

_____

_____

_____

_____

7. For additional study, read each of the following verses and comment on what each of them means to you.

   Ephesians 2:8–9

   Romans 8:35–39

   Titus 3:5

   Philippians 1:6

8. Daily Bible study helps you to grow in your relationship with Jesus Christ. For your spiritual encouragement, be faithful in reading the Bible. Ask your helper what Bible books or chapters he or she recommends for you. Read your Bible daily.

9. First John 5:11–13 reminds the believer that God guarantees eternal life. It is a Bible passage on assurance of salvation. Commit 1 John 5:11–13 to memory. Then repeat the passage aloud to a Christian friend.

Follow-Up 3: For the Bible Tells Me So

My name is _____.

My helper's name and phone number are _____

_____.

Please read the following paragraph aloud.

The person who receives Jesus Christ as Savior is spiritually reborn (John 3:3, 7). Believers begin spiritual life as "newborn babes" (1 Peter 2:2). It is natural for babies to grow and develop. Believers must "grow in grace and in the knowledge of our Lord and Savior Jesus Christ" (2 Peter 3:18). Spiritual growth requires spiritual nourishment (food). The believer's primary source of nourishment is the Bible. The purpose of this study is to discover from scripture how believers can grow through regular nourishment from God's Word. Read the scripture references given. Then write your answers in the spaces provided.

1. How can believers grow in Jesus Christ?

   Spiritual "newborn babies" need the sincere _____ of God's Word that growth might result (1 Peter 2:2).

   When spiritual babies become more mature, they can understand more difficult passages of scripture. These scripture passages are called the strong _____ of God's Word (Hebrews 5:14).

   God's Word is _____ (John 17:17).

   God gave the Bible. It is profitable for _____, what is right; for _____, what is not right; for _____, how to get right; and for _____ in righteousness, how to stay right (2 Timothy 3:16).

   Believers must be diligent to be workmen who are not _____, rightly interpreting the word of truth (2 Timothy 2:15).

   Do you drink milk? Why?

   Do you eat food? Why?

We drink milk because it is good for us. We eat food because our bodies need it to be strong and to grow. We read and study God's Word, the Bible, because it is good for us. It helps us grow spiritually and to be a stronger believer in Christ.

2. How can believers communicate with or talk to God?

God shares His mind with believers through scripture. Believers talk to God through prayer. Prayer is talking to God. Look up the following passages of scripture, and fill in the blanks.

Paul said to _____ _____ _____ (1 Thessalonians 5:17).

Through prayer, believers have immediate access to God. Believers can pray anytime and anywhere.

Jesus said to _____, _____, and _____ and it shall be opened to us (Matthew 7:7).

Picture someone knocking at your front door. The individual wants something from you. The person sought you out to provide something. The person keeps knocking until you answer the door. That is what God wants you to do when you approach Him in prayer. Keep on asking, keep on seeking, and keep on knocking until God answers your prayer.

Believers must ask in the _____ of Jesus Christ (John 14:13).

The name of Jesus is the summary statement of all that Jesus is. By closing your prayer, "In Jesus's name, Amen," God's Son becomes involved in your prayer; He identifies with your prayer. Always include Jesus in your prayer because Jesus is God talking to God about you.

3. For what should believers pray?

    Believers should pray for daily _____
    (Matthew 6:11), for protection from being led into
    _____ (Matthew 6:12), and for
    deliverance from _____ (Matthew 6:13).

    Daily "bread" speaks of God providing our daily needs, which includes our daily food.

    Believers should pray for _____ in dealing with the trials of life (James 1:5).

    Paul prayed for other believers (Romans 1:9). He asked other believers to _____ for him (Romans 15:30–32).

    Believers should pray that others would _____ on Jesus Christ in response to His Word being spoken (John 17:20).

4. Begin a personal prayer diary. Include columns to record requests, the date the requests were made, how God answered those requests, and the date God answered each request.

    <u>Date</u> <u>Prayer Request</u> <u>God's Answer</u> <u>Date God Answered</u>

5. David wrote, "Delight thyself also in the Lord: and He shall give thee the desires of thine heart" (Psalm 34:4). Believers must want what God wants. The will of God is a key essential to answered prayer. For additional study, look up the following scripture passages in God's Word (the Bible). Then draw lines connecting the following scripture passages to the appropriate references.

The Bible is a weapon known as "the sword of the Spirit."	Psalm 119:105
The Bible is a "lamp" unto our feet and a "light" unto our path.	Ephesians 6:17
The Bible is a "looking glass."	Psalm 126:5–6
The Bible is eternal and will "never pass away."	James 1:23
The Bible is a "precious seed."	Matthew 24:35
The Bible is, "sweeter than honey."	Jeremiah 23:29
The Bible is like "fire" to your soul.	Psalm 19:10
The Bible is "milk," providing spiritual nourishment.	1 Peter 2:2

6. For your encouragement, read your Bible daily, pray daily, and memorize, in order, the names of the books of the New Testament. A list of the New Testament

books, in order, is found in the "Contents" of your Bible as well as below.

Matthew	Ephesians	Hebrews
Mark	Philippians	James
Luke	Colossians	1 Peter
John	1 Thessalonians	2 Peter
Acts	2 Thessalonians	1 John
Romans	1 Timothy	2 John
1 Corinthians	2 Timothy	3 John
2 Corinthians	Titus	Jude
Galatians	Philemon	Revelation
		(27 in all)

Follow-Up 4: Little Ones to Him Belong

My name is _____.

My helper's name and phone number are _____

_____.

Please read the following paragraph aloud.

Most people like to feel accepted or to belong. Because we belong to Jesus, God accepts us and loves us through His Son, the beloved One who is Jesus (Ephesians 1:6b). You are a 'King's kid' with all the privileges and the responsibilities of a natural-born child. Because we are saved, what does God expect from us?

The purpose of this study is to describe your spiritual privileges and responsibilities. Read the scripture references given. Then write your answers in the spaces provided.

1. People who are saved (believers) have the privilege of telling others about Jesus Christ.

   The practice of telling others about Jesus Christ is called witnessing (Acts 1:8). If Jesus Christ is worth having, He is worth sharing with others. The Bible has much to say about what we say about Jesus. Look up the following verses, and fill in the blanks.

   Believers must be ready to give an _____ to every man who asks a reason of the _____ that is in you (1 Peter 3:15).

   Proverbs 11:30 teaches that "he who wins _____ is wise."

   The believer who goes forth with God-given sincerity, bearing the precious seed of the gospel, will doubtless come again with _____, bringing his _____ (new converts) with him (Psalm 126:6).

   Acts 1:8 indicates that witnessing for Jesus Christ includes the following four geographical locations: _____ (your community), _____ (your county and state), _____ (your country), and the _____ _____ (internationally to the continents beyond).

The believer has the responsibility to witness to _____ men, "of what thou hast seen and heard" (Acts 22:15).

Since Christ is worth having, He is worth sharing with others. Because you are saved, tell someone others about Jesus.

2. Believers have the privilege of waiting for the return of the Lord.

God's true church is taken to heaven in the rapture (1 Thessalonians 4:13–17).[4] The promise of the rapture gives comfort to true believers (1 Thessalonians 4:18). Then we who are, "alive and remain shall be _____ _____ (raptured) together with them in the clouds to meet the _____ in the air; and so shall we ever be with the _____" (1 Thessalonians 4:17).

Jesus Christ has prepared a home in heaven for those who know Him as Savior. His promise is, "I will _____ again" (John 14:3).

Believers look for "that blessed hope" that is the glorious _____ of our Lord and Savior Jesus Christ (Titus 2:13).

---

[4] Although the English word "rapture" does not appear in the King James Version English translation, it is from a Latin term that means "to catch up" or "be caught up."

3. Believers have the privilege of pleasing Jesus Christ. This involves guarding against sin and temptation.

When believers are tempted to do wrong, God provides a way of escape. "There hath no _____ taken you but such as is _____ to man; but God is _____, Who will not suffer you to be _____ above that ye are able, but will with the temptation also make a _____ of escape that ye might be able to bear it" (1 Corinthians 10:13).

Temptation is a desire to think or do something that does not please God. The temptation is not the sin. The sin is falling for the temptation and doing the wrong action or thinking the wrong thought. Although sin includes such behaviors as disobedience to parents, lying, stealing, and bad thoughts, sin is more than that. Sin is doing, saying, or thinking anything that is against God or contrary to scripture. It is anything that does not please God. Guard your mind by placing Jesus at the door of your mind (thoughts) and heart (desires), so you do not fall into sin. As a person thinks in his or her heart (mind), so that person is (Proverbs 23:7). Because thoughts break out into actions, be careful to think thoughts that please God.

Are you committed to thinking thoughts that please God?

_____ Yes   _____ No

Is it your desire to overcome temptation in your life?

_____ Yes   _____ No

4. The Bible provides help in determining whether certain activities, attitudes, and thoughts are right or wrong. With the assistance of your helper, match the following scripture verses with the appropriate statements. Anytime you are not sure that your choice is the right one, ask one or more of these questions of your situation, choice, or decision.

Will it glorify God?	1 Corinthians 10:31
Can it be done for the Lord?	Colossians 3:17
Can it be done in the name of the Lord?	Colossians 3:23
Is it of that evil world system that opposes all that God represents?	1 Thessalonians 5:22
Are you in doubt about it?	1 John 2:15
Is it good in its appearance?	Romans 14:23
Would it hinder a fellow believer?	2 Corinthians 6:14a
Will it form an unequal yoke with an unbeliever?	Romans 14:21
Could it become my master?	1 Corinthians 6:12b

Is it God's will for my life?   James 4:15

Am I willing to face it in   2 Corinthians 5:10
the judgment? Would I want
to be involved in this activity
when Jesus Christ comes again?

Do I want to reap the fruit of   Galatians 6:7
this activity in my future life
or in the lives of those I love?

5. Believers have the responsibility to attend a Bible-preaching church.

   Is church attendance important? _____ Yes   _____ No

   Believers are not to _____ the assembling
   of ourselves _____ as the manner
   of some is, but instead [believers are] to encourage one
   another through faithful church attendance, because of
   the Lord's return (see Hebrews 10:25).

6. Believers have a responsibility to be baptized by immersion
   following salvation.

   Is baptism a step of obedience to the command of Jesus
   Christ (Matthew 28:18–20)?

   _____ Yes _____ No

The Bible records the instructions of Peter to a group of new Christians: "and he _____ them to be _____ in the name of the Lord Jesus" (Acts 10:48).

How important is obedience to the commands of Jesus Christ (John 15:14)?

_____ Important   _____ Not Important

A helpful class on believer's baptism is offered at the church. Why not arrange with the pastor to attend this class?

7. Believers have a responsibility to observe the Table of the Lord (communion).

Who instituted the Table of the Lord (Matthew 26:26–28)? _____ _____.

The bread used in the communion service is symbolic of the _____ of Jesus Christ, which was given for believers at Calvary (1 Corinthians 11:24). The cup, filled with grape juice, is symbolic of the _____ Jesus Christ shed on the cross for forgiveness of sins (1 Corinthians 11:25). Communion is observed in _____ of what Jesus Christ did at Calvary (1 Corinthians 11:24–25).

8. Believers have the responsibility to join a local church (church membership).

   Acts 2:41–42 lists a sequence of three important events in the lives of new believers. First, they gladly _____ the Word (salvation), then they were _____ (by immersion following salvation), and finally, they were _____ (joined as members) to the local church. These early believers formed a local fellowship. They became members of a local church (Acts 1:15).

   In review, in what three events did the new believers participate?

   a. Salvation
   b. B
   c. Church Membership

Following the successful completion of baptism class, the church offers a class on local church membership. Ask your pastor when this class meets. You are invited to participate in this class.

9. For your encouragement, review the truths presented in the following lessons.

   "Follow-Up 1: *Jesus Loves Me* reviews what the Bible says about our salvation experience.
   "Follow-Up 2: *This I Know* tells us what God says about your assurance of salvation.

"Follow-Up 3: *For the Bible Tells Me So* shares truths about God's Word, the Bible.

"Follow-Up 4: *Little Ones to Him Belong* reminds us of the privileges and responsibilities we have as believers.

Review

10. For your growth, continue to read your Bible, pray daily, and memorize scripture passages relating to your walk—your relationship—with Christ. Also, memorize in order the names of the books of the Old Testament. A listing of the Old Testament books is found in the "Contents" of your Bible and as follows.

Genesis	Ecclesiastes
Exodus	Song of Solomon
Leviticus	Isaiah
Numbers	Jeremiah
Deuteronomy	Lamentations
Joshua	Ezekiel
Judges	Daniel
Ruth	Hosea
1 Samuel	Joel
2 Samuel	Amos
1 Kings	Obadiah
2 Kings	Jonah
1 Chronicles	Micah
2 Chronicles	Nahum
Ezra	Habakkuk
Nehemiah	Zephaniah
Esther	Haggai

Job	Zechariah
Psalms	Malachi
Proverbs	(39 in all)

Praise God! Jesus loves you! He knows! He loves! He cares!

Answers to the Follow-Up Sessions

(For the Discipler)

Follow-Up 1: Jesus Loves Me

Romans 3:23	All
John 14:6	Way, Truth, Life
Romans 6:23a	Wages
Select one:	_____ Heaven
	_____ Hell
Romans 5:8	Love
John 1:12	Receive
Fill in the date of your salvation (the date you were saved):	_____, _____
Are you sure that you are saved?	Yes/No

All other answers should be reviewed on an individual basis by the discipler with his or her disciple.

Follow-Up 2: This I Know

1 John 5:13	Eternal Life
John 10:28	Perish
Romans 8:16	Spirit/Children
1 Peter 1:5	God
Are you sure that you are saved beyond this life?	Yes/No
John 3:16	Fill in your name
Have you received Jesus Christ as your personal Lord and Savior?	Yes/No
Are your sins forgiven?	Yes/No
How do you know that you have eternal life?	(See the study for the answer.)

Follow-Up 3: For the Bible Tells Me So

1 Peter 2:2	Milk
Hebrews 5:14	Meat
John 17:17	Truth
2 Timothy 3:16	Doctrine, Reproof, Correction, Instruction
2 Timothy 2:15	Ashamed
1 Thessalonians 5:17	Pray Without Ceasing
Matthew 7:7	Ask, Seek, Knock
John 14:13	Name
Matthew 6:11–13	Bread/Daily Needs, Temptation, Evil
James 1:5	Wisdom
Romans 15:30–32	Pray
John 17:20	Believe

Matching

The Bible is a weapon.	Ephesians 6:17
The Bible is a lamp.	Psalm 119:105
The Bible is a looking glass.	James 1:23
The Bible is eternal.	Matthew 24:35
The Bible is a precious seed.	Psalm 126:5–6
The Bible is sweeter than honey.	Psalm 19:10
The Bible is fire.	Jeremiah 23:29
The Bible is milk.	1 Peter 2:2

Follow-Up 4: Little Ones to Him Belong

1 Peter 3:15	Answer, Hope
Proverbs 11:30	Souls
Psalm 126:6	Rejoicing, Sheaves
Acts 1:8	Jerusalem, Judea, Samaria, Uttermost Parts of the World
Acts 22:15	All
1 Thessalonians 4:17	Caught Up, Lord, Lord
John 14:3	Come
Titus 2:13	Appearing
1 Corinthians 10:13	Temptation, Common, Faithful, Tempted, Way
Commitment to please God/Desire to overcome temptation:	___Yes ___No ___Yes ___No

Matching

Will it glorify God?	1 Corinthians 10:31
Can it be done for the Lord?	Colossians 3:23
Can it be in the Lord's name?	Colossians 3:17
Is it of the evil world system?	1 John 2:15
Are you in doubt about it?	Romans 14:23
Is it good in its appearance?	1 Thessalonians 5:22
Would it hinder a believer?	Romans 14:21
Will it form an unequal yoke?	2 Corinthians 6:14
Could it become my master?	1 Corinthians 6:12b
Is it God's will?	James 4:15
Am I willing to be judged for it?	2 Corinthians 5:10
Do I want to reap its fruit?	Galatians 6:7

Hebrews 10:25	Forsake, Together
Matthew 28:18-20	Yes/No
Acts 10:48	Commanded, Baptized
John 15:14	Important/Not Important
	Jesus Christ
Matthew 26:26–28	Body, Blood, Remembrance
1 Corinthians 11:24–25	Received,
	Baptized, Added,
Acts 2:41–42	Salvation, Baptism, Membership

Addendum:

How to Study the Bible,
Questions and Answers

How to Study the Bible

A disciple is one who follows Jesus Christ. A Christ-follower who spent daily time with Jesus wrote, "But grow in grace and in the knowledge of our Lord and Savior Jesus Christ. To Him be glory both now and forever. Amen" (2 Peter 3:18). For the purpose of spiritual growth, all believers need to study the Bible. A thorough study of God's Word strengthens the believer's trust in God (grace) and acquaints believers with the truths of God (knowledge). Time spent in the Bible and in prayer is called a believer's devotional life.

Paul was a Christ-follower who spent time daily with Jesus. Paul wrote, "All Scripture is given by inspiration of God, and is profitable for doctrine (what is right), for reproof (what is not right), for correction (how to get right), and for instruction in righteousness (how to stay right): That the man of God may be perfect (mature and complete), thoroughly furnished unto all good works" (2 Timothy 3:16–17). The purpose of this study is to answer five questions concerning a believer's devotional life (quiet time with God).[5]

---

[5] The lesson "How to Study the Bible" is taken from "Q—Quiet Time" in the Keith D. Pisani's book, *Spiritual Lessons for Growing Believers*, which is published by WestBow Press and is available through the publisher and the author's website: www.keithpisaniministries.com.

1. Why Should Believers Have a Quiet Time with God?

Daily Bible study benefits believers for the following reasons. Look up the following scripture passages. Describe the benefit a study of God's Word provides for the believer. Refer to the listings at the end of this session for this study's answers.

Joshua 1:6–8   (_____) in God's Word is the key to success

Joshua had one option for God's people Israel: Win. Defeat meant annihilation. Joshua wrote,

> Be strong and of a good courage: for unto this people shalt thou divide for an inheritance the land, which I sware unto their fathers to give them. Only be thou strong and very courageous, that thou mayest observe to do according to all the law, which Moses my servant commanded thee: turn not from it to the right hand or to the left, that thou mayest prosper withersoever thou goest. This book of the law shall not depart out of thy mouth; but thou shalt meditate therein day and night, that thou mayest observe to do according to all that is written therein: for then thou shalt make thy way prosperous, and then thou shalt have good success. (Joshua 1:8)

The wisdom derived from God's Word gives the believer an edge in analyzing situations and actions. It is the key to winning or losing in life.

Psalm 119:9, 11   It keeps a believer from (_____)

"Wherewithal shall a young man cleanse his way? By taking heed thereto according to Thy Word. With my whole heart have I sought Thee: O let me not wander from Thy commandments. Thy Word have I hid in mine heart, that I might not sin against Thee." The term "hid" means to "treasure up" as a priceless possession. Either sin will keep the believer from the Bible, or the Bible will keep the believer from sin. Study God's Word. It helps keep the believer separated from bad thoughts and wrongdoings.

Psalm 119:105, 130   It shines a (_____) on hard-to-understand matters

"Thy Word is a lamp unto my feet, and a light unto my path. The entrance of Thy words giveth light; it giveth understanding unto the simple" (Psalm 119:105, 130). An Old Testament oil "lamp" was worn on the toe of a person's sandal. It gave light for one step at a time. A "light" was a torch or other device that gave illumination for an extended length of time and distance. God's Word penetrates the darkness. It provides light for the believer's journey through life.

Proverbs 2:1–5   It provides a source of spiritual (_____)

My son, if thou wilt receive my words, and hide my commandments with thee; So that thou incline thine ear unto wisdom, and apply thine heart to understanding; Yea, if thou criest after knowledge, and liftest up thy voice for understanding; If thou seekest her as silver, and searchest for her as for hid treasures; Then shalt thou understand the fear of the Lord, and find the knowledge of God. (Proverbs 2:1–5)

One possession every believer needs is spiritual discernment. The source of discernment is the wisdom of God. Wisdom comes from God (James 1:2–4) and His Word (Proverbs 1:1–7). To obtain the wisdom given by God, believers must study God's Word. Applied wisdom takes the guesswork out of life.

Jeremiah 15:16 <u>It brings God's (   ) to the believer's life</u>

"Thy words were found, and I did eat them; and Thy Word was unto me the joy and rejoicing of mine heart: for I am called by Thy name, O Lord God of hosts" (Jeremiah 15:16). When Jeremiah found the scroll of God's Word, he took it into his system and digested its truths. The spiritual nourishment he received changed his life; when it hit his stomach, it made *the* difference in his life. To receive nourishment from God's Word, the believer must drink the milk (1 Peter 2:2) and eat the meat (Hebrews 5:14) of God's Word. Live on the strength of the Word.

Acts 17:10–14 <u>It adds (   ) to life</u>

And the brethren immediately sent away Paul and Silas by night unto Berea: who coming thither went into the synagogue of the Jews. These were more noble than those in Thessalonica, in that they received the Word with all readiness of mind, and searched the Scriptures daily, whether those things were so. Therefore many of them believed; also of honorable women which were Greeks, and of men, not a few. But when the Jews of Thessalonica had knowledge that the Word of God was preached of Paul at Berea, they came thither also, and stirred up the people. (Acts 17:10–14)

God's Word, publicly proclaimed, makes unbelievers nervous and angry. "Upset" ("upset" used as an adjective) people "upset" (used here as a verb) people. Even so, the Bereans remained steadfast in their love for the Word. Presenters who dilute the message of scripture and replace it with popular opinions and philosophy do the church a major disservice. Only God's Word brings eternal security to a person's life. Make time for God by making time for His Word.

1 Peter 2:2   It results in spiritual (_____)

"As newborn babes, desire the sincere milk of the word, that ye may grow thereby" (1 Peter 2:2). Physical bodies that remain the size of babies (people who never grow) are aberrations. Believers are born to grow. Christians who remain spiritual infants are immature in their faith. How much spiritual growth have you experienced since you were saved? What stunts your spiritual growth? Have you continued to grow, or does your personal growth chart indicate that you have "shrunk" in your faith?

| 2 Timothy 2:15 | It allows believers to (_____) God's command to (_____) His Word |

"Study to shew thyself approved unto God, a workman that needeth not to be ashamed, rightly dividing the Word of truth" (2 Timothy 2:15). To "rightly divide" means to "cut the furrow straight." There is one proper interpretation of God's Word, God's interpretation (2 Peter 1:19–21). When studying God's Word, compare scripture with scripture. This allows for a more consistent interpretation of Bible passages. In life, instead of asking, "What would Jesus do?" ask, "What does the Bible say?" What Jesus would do is open to speculation. What the Bible says is black ink on white paper. It is clear.

In a verse titled "My Bible and I," a poet wrote,

> We've traveled together, my Bible and I,
> Through all kinds of weather, with smile or with sigh!
> In sorrow or sunshine, in tempest or calm!
> Thy friendship unchanging, my lamp and my psalm.
>
> Oh, no, my dear Bible, exponent of light!
> Thou sword of the Spirit, put error to flight!
> And still through life's journey, until my last sigh,

We'll travel together, my Bible and I.[6]

A quiet time is a time of prayer, study, meditation, and application of God's Word. To have a quiet time, the believer must have a place (Mark 1:35), a plan (Luke 14:28), and an available period of time (Psalm 119:147–148). The purpose of this study is to answer four questions about a personal quiet time with God, with emphasis on the believer's time spent in God's Word. (For insights on prayer, see "Follow-Up 3: For the Bible Tells Me So."

2. What Should Believers Include When Having a Quiet Time with God?

Pick up your Bible. How securely can you grasp it with one finger? How securely can you grasp it with two fingers? You cannot grasp your Bible securely until you get a firm grip with your whole hand. How should believers grab hold of the Word? A hand illustration is an easy-to-remember training tool on getting a firm grasp on the Bible. Draw an outline of your hand on a blank piece of paper. Then label each finger with the five key terms listed in this study.[7] The following are five methods believers can use to learn from the Scriptures. Refer to the addendum at the end of this study for this session's answers.

---

[6] As quoted in Eleanor Doan's, *Speaker's Sourcebook*, (Grand Rapids: Zondervan, 1960), 34–35.

[7] The hand illustration is an adaptation of a popular training tool appearing often in the public sector.

Romans 10:17   (H_____) the Word

Paul wrote, "So then faith cometh by hearing, and hearing by the Word of God" (Romans 10:17). People retain 5 percent of what they hear. Hearing is the least effective method of retention. The weakest finger (the pinkie) represents hearing. Hearing the Word from trained teachers and godly pastors provides valuable insights into God's Word. Believers can hear the Word in church (preaching service, Sunday school, small groups, Bible studies), on electronic devices (over the air, over media connections), and through word of mouth.

Revelation 1:3   (R_____) the Word

John wrote, "Blessed is he that readeth, and they that hear the words of this prophecy, and keep those things that are written therein: for the time is at hand" (Revelation 1:3). Reading gives an overall picture of the Bible. Reading is an essential ingredient in experiencing quality quiet time. People retain 15 percent of what they read. Reading is represented by the ring (fourth) finger. Believers are guaranteed a blessing from God when they read God's Word.

Acts 17:11   (S_____) the Word

Luke reported that the believers at Berea, "searched the Scriptures daily, as to whether those things were so" (Acts 17:11). Studying requires a greater investment of time and results in an increase in Bible knowledge. Most people retain 35 percent of what they study. This method is represented by the middle finger.

Psalm 119:9, 11   (M   ) the Word

The psalmist wrote, "Wherewithal shall a young man cleanse his way? By taking heed thereto according to Thy word … Thy word have I hid in my heart that I might not sin against Thee" (Psalm 119:9, 11). "Hid" means to "treasure up and count as precious." For the believer who memorizes God's Word, the Holy Spirit brings to mind appropriate verses to help the believer through times of trial or temptation. Scripture memory stimulates meaningful meditation. People who consistently review what they memorized remember 100 percent of the memorized passages. The index finger, which is the strongest finger, represents scripture memorization. How much of scripture have you memorized?

Psalm 1:1–2   (M   ) on God's Word

David wrote, "Blessed is the man who walketh not in the counsel of the ungodly, nor standeth in the way of sinners, nor sitteth in the seat of the scornful. But his delight is in the law of the Lord; and in His law doth he meditate both day and night" (Psalm 1:1–2). "Meditation" was used by farmers of cows chewing their cud and of Roman senators reviewing their speeches before they were delivered. Meditation is reviewing what the believer has learned. It is the secret to spiritual prosperity (Joshua 1:8). Paul wrote that believers should, "give [themselves] wholly to meditation; that his profiting might appear to all" (1 Timothy 4:15). Meditation results in inner growth. It should accompany the other four methods of learning. This is why the thumb represents meditation. Meditation allows God's Word to transform the life of the believer.

Some like entertainment or sports. Others read the stock pages. If believers were as interested in God's Word as some people are interested in entertainment, sports schedules, or other reports, society would be a better place.

3. What Questions Should a Believer Ask When Studying God's Word?

Paul wrote, "Study to shew thyself approved unto God, a workman that needeth not to be ashamed, rightly dividing the Word of truth" (2 Timothy 2:15). Just as reporters ask journalistic questions about the events they cover, believers can ask questions of God's Word. These questions help the believer determine the meaning and proper application of God's Word to his or her life. Select a passage of scripture (Psalm 23 or some other passage), and ask the following questions of that passage. (Please look in the listings at the end of this study for this session's answers.)

What was the author's intended _m_____?

Every text has a purpose and a meaning intended by its author. No passage is of any "private interpretation" (2 Peter 1:21). God wants believers to understand His Word. Believers should seek to understand the mind-set of the author. In Psalm 23. the author wants the reader to appreciate the relationship of a compassionate shepherd with his sheep.

What is the immediate and wider _c_   of the passage?

How does the passage fit into the passages that surround it? The ultimate context is the entire Bible. The general context is the book in which the passage is found. The immediate context applies to the passages immediately before and immediately after the one being studied. In Psalm 23, the context is the crucifixion of God's Lamb, as pictured in Psalm 22, and the sovereign reign of Jesus (Psalm 24). Psalms 22–24 are a trio of chapters describing various aspects of Jesus Christ's death, ministry, and life.

What _t_   of passage is being studied?

The Bible includes a variety of literary types. It includes history, prophecy, proverbs, parables, literal, narrative, allegorical, and other types of writings. Some passages have figures of speech. Other passages say, "This is that." The style and type of writing are important to an understanding of God's Word. Psalm 23 is one song in the hymn book of Israel. It is described as "wisdom" literature and is a teaching passage.

What are the _h_   , _g_   , and _c_   contexts of the passage?

The Bible was not written in a vacuum. It was written in a context of history, geography, and culture. It is important to understand the text in the same way the original listener or reader understood the text. When reading a parable, see the truths as Christ's listeners would see those truths. When reading Psalm 23, it is important to interpret the psalm in the context of how a shepherd would understand the writing. Historically and geographically, it took place during the early life of David, outside of Bethlehem in the shepherd's fields, where a valley passes between two hills. Culturally, David was Jewish living in an agricultural (nonindustrial) society.

What is the structure of the passage's g_____
_____ (its hermeneutic)?

What is the subject, the verb, and the object? Is the subject a person or a thing? What is the tense and voice of the verb? Are there words associated with the subject, verb, and object (adjectives and adverbs)? In what way is the passage connected to previous passages and other passages in its context? How does the passage relate to the theme of the context? Good Bible students pay attention to detail. Some Bible students diagram passages when they study God's Word. This allows the student to see how each word is connected to the other words in the passage. In Psalm 23, highlights include the present tense of Psalm 23:1 ("The Lord *is* my shepherd") and the personal aspects of the relationship between the shepherd and the psalmist, knowing that the psalmist was a shepherd as well. Then the words and phrases of the psalm should be studied individually (In Psalm 23, describe the "green pastures" in a barren landscape; "stilled waters" are the only waters a sheep will drink; To "restore" is to turn around as in repentance; How does a shepherd lead: from ahead or from behind?; Ask: what is the identity and location of the valley?; What fears does the sheep experience? Who is with the psalmist?; What are the functions of the rod and the staff in relation to sheep?; Describe the table, the guests, and the anointing; What kind of traveling companions do goodness and mercy make?; and where is the psalmist now?) From the grammatical structure and its applications, an outline of the passage can be derived. Also, remember this: Often, the action verb (in the passage) leads the reader to the main thought. Many teaching outlines begin with the verbs.

What does the _r_____ of the _B_____ say about the passage being studied?

Believers should never read a passage of scripture in isolation from the remainder of the Bible. Believers should compare scripture with scripture. God is consistent in what He presents. Refuse to interpret scripture based on personal experiences; interpret personal experiences based on the scripture. Allow the Bible to determine its own meaning. God's will never contradicts His revealed Word. God remains consistent with His Word.

Every time you study God's Word, "pray in" God's texts. Do more than pray for insight. Pray that you can properly apply God's truths to your daily life. Prayer allows God to apply the texts to the daily life of believers.

4. What Are the Benefits of Studying God's Word?

In what ways does God's Word benefit the believer? Look up the following passages, match each passage to the corresponding truth, and if you have the companion workbook, comment on the personal benefit you gain from studying God's Word in the spaces provided. (This is a non exhaustive list. Please look in the listings at the end of this study to check your answers.)

Psalm 19:7–11 _____   A. It brings new life (conversion) to the soul.

Psalm 119:9, 11 _____   B. It builds up the believer in the faith.

Psalm 119:99 _____   C. It helps the believer know and understand God's truth.

Psalm 119:105 _____   D. It helps the believer know right from wrong.

Matthew 4:4 _____   E. It keeps the believer from sin.

John 8:32 _____   F. It gives direction and guidance to the believer's life.

John 17:17 _____ G. It is spiritual bread (food) for the soul (see also 1 Peter 2:2; Hebrews 5:14).

Acts 17:11 _____ H. It makes the believer a better worker for God.

Acts 20:32 _____ I. It reveals who God (Jesus) is.

Ephesians 3:19 _____ J. It gives insight into what is fact and what is false.

2 Timothy 2:15 _____ K. It liberates the believer.

Hebrews 5:14 _____ L. It sanctifies believers (sets believers apart from sin).

The believer who wants to live a life consistent with God's character will study God's Word. Do it daily.

5. What Study Helps Are Available for Use in Studying God's Word?

A variety of study aids are available to help the believer study God's Word. They include the following (this is a non exhaustive list).

The Bible, resource materials from Christian bookstores and church libraries, Bible concordances, Bible dictionaries, Bible encyclopedias, Bible handbooks, Bible customs books, Bible maps, language helps, commentaries, additional reference books, theology books, hymnals, worship guides, seminars, workshops, conferences, Bible study manuals, electronic media, fellowship groups, Bible studies, language helps, and internet and website materials.

Believers can study God's Word anytime and anywhere. Believers can study a word, a phrase, a sentence, a verse, a chapter, or a book. Bible study can be private, with the family before or after a meal, or with a group. When studying the Bible, read it through (get something specific), pray it in (apply it), write it down (mark your Bible or keep a notebook), work it out (in daily life), and pass it on (tell others). Be creative and consistent with the content of God's Word.

Of the Bible, an author wrote,

This book contains the mind of God, the state of man, the way of salvation, the doom of sinners, and the happiness of believers. Its doctrines are holy, its precepts are binding, its histories are true, and its decisions are immutable. Read it to be wise, believe it to be safe, and practice it to be holy. It contains light to direct you, food to support you, and comfort to cheer you. It is the traveler's map, the pilgrim's staff, the pilot's compass, the soldier's sword, and the Christian's charter. Here Paradise is restored, heaven opened, and the gates of hell disclosed. Christ is the grand subject, our good its design, and the glory of

God its end. It should fill the memory, rule the heart, and guide the feet. Read it slowly, frequently, and prayerfully. It is a mine of wealth, a paradise of glory, and a river of pleasure. It is given to you in life, will be opened at the judgment, and will be remembered forever. It involves the highest responsibility, will reward the greatest labor, and condemns all who trifle with its sacred contents.[8]

Get everything you can from God's Word. A study of the Bible will bless your life.

For your encouragement, participate in the following exercises (see the companion workbook that accompanies this study).

1. Conduct Bible studies in the following passage types:

   Allegorical/Prophecy (Matthew 24–25)

   Narrative (1 Samuel 17)

   Literal/Expository (Ephesians 1:3–14)

2. Compare scripture with scripture on the following topics:

   Marriage (Genesis 1:21–25; 2:20; Ephesians 5:21–33)

   The Home (Deuteronomy 6:4–9; Proverbs 22:6; Ephesians 6:1–4)

---

[8] Priscilla Howe, "The Bible," as quoted in *Uncle Ben's Quotebook* (Grand Rapids: Baker Book House, 1976), 57.

A Relationship of Grace compared to a Religion of Works (Galatians)

3. Conduct some personal Bible studies by applying the information provided in this study.

Study 1: What God Does with Sin

Psalm 32:1

Psalm 32:2

Psalm 103:12

Isaiah 1:18

Isaiah 38:17

Isaiah 43:25

Isaiah 55:7

Micah 7:19

Matthew 26:28

John 1:29

Hebrews 1:3

1 John 1:9

Study 2: Bible Be's

Be_____   Job 22:21

Be_____   Joshua 1:6

Be_____   Matthew 5:48

Be_____   Matthew 14:27

Be_____   Ephesians 4:32

Be_____   James 5:7

Be_____   1 Peter 5:5

Be_____   1 Peter 5:5

Be_____   1 Peter 5:8

Be_____   2 Peter 3:14

Study: Some Sure Things

Thou shalt surely _____.   Genesis 2:17

Be sure your _____ will find   Numbers 32:23
you out.

The _____ of God   2 Timothy 2:19
standeth sure.

The sure word of the _____ of God.   2 Peter 1:19

Surely I _____ quickly.   Revelation 22:20

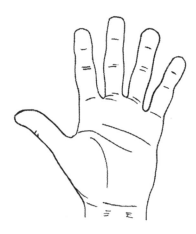

The following are five methods believers can use to learn from the Scriptures. Use the key terms in this section to complete the hand illustration.

Romans 10:17   _____the Word.

Revelation 1:3   _____the Word.

Acts 17:11   _____the Word.

Psalm 119:9, 11)   _____the Word.

Psalm 1:1–2   _____on God's Word.

Answers to the
"How to Study the Bible" Session

(For the discipler)

1. Why Should Believers Have a Quiet Time of Study/Devotion with God?

Joshua 1:6–8	Meditation
Psalm 119:9, 11	Sin
Psalm 119:105, 130	Light
Proverbs 2:1–5	Wisdom
Jeremiah 15:16	Joy
Acts 17:10–14	Stability
1 Peter 2:2	Growth
2 Timothy 2:15	Obey/Study

2. What Should Believers Include When Having a Quiet Time of Study/Devotion with God?

Hand Illustration

Romans 10:17	Hear the Word.
Revelation 1:3	Read the Word.
Acts 17:11	Study the Word.
Psalm 119:9, 11	Memorize the Word.
Psalm 1:1–2	Meditate on God's Word.

3. What Questions Should a Believer Ask When Studying God's Word?

What was the author's intended <u>meaning</u>?

What are the immediate and wider <u>context</u>s of the passage?

What <u>type</u> of passage is being studied?

What is the <u>historical</u>, <u>geographical</u>, and <u>cultural</u> contexts of the passage?

What is the <u>grammatical</u> <u>structure</u> of the passage (its hermeneutic)?

What does the <u>rest</u> of the <u>Bible</u> say about the passage being studied?

4. What Are the Benefits of Studying God's Word?

In what ways does God's Word benefit the believer? Look up the following passages, match each passage to the corresponding truth, and if you have the companion workbook, comment on the personal benefit you gain from studying God's Word in the spaces provided (this is a non exhaustive list).

Psalm 19:7–11   _____A_____   A. It brings new life (conversion) to the soul.

Psalm 119:9, 11   _____E_____   B. It builds up the believer in the faith.

Psalm 119:99	C	C.	It helps the believer know and understand God's truth.
Psalm 119:105	F	D.	It helps the believer know right from wrong.
Matthew 4:4	G	E.	It keeps the believer from sin.
John 8:32	K	F.	It gives direction and guidance to the believer's life.
John 17:17	L	G.	It is spiritual bread (food) for the soul (see also 1 Peter 2:2; Hebrews 5:14).
Acts 17:11	J	H.	It makes the believer a better worker for God.
Acts 20:32	B	I.	It reveals Who God (Jesus) is.
Ephesians 3:19	I	J.	It gives insight into what is fact and what is false.
2 Timothy 2:15	H	K.	It liberates the believer.
Hebrews 5:14	D	L.	It sanctifies believers (sets believers apart).

5. What Bible Study Helps Are Available for Use in Studying God's Word?

The Bible, resource materials from Christian bookstores and church libraries, Bible concordances, Bible dictionaries, Bible encyclopedias, Bible handbooks, Bible customs books, Bible maps, language helps, commentaries, additional reference books, theology books, hymnals, worship guides, seminars, workshops, conferences, Bible study manuals, electronic media, fellowship groups, Bible studies, language helps, internet and website materials, and other resources and aids.

Exercises

1. Conduct Bible studies in the following passage types:

   Allegorical/Prophecy (Matthew 24–25)—Christ's Olivet discourse

   Narrative (1 Samuel 17)—David and Goliath

   Literal/Expository (Ephesians 1:3–14)—Paul's doctrinal teaching(s)

2. Compare scripture with scripture on the following topics.

   Marriage (Genesis 1:21–25; 2:20; Ephesians 5:21–33)

   The Home (Deuteronomy 6:4–9; Proverbs 22:6; Ephesians 6:1–4)

A Relationship of Grace compared to a Religion of Works
(Galatians)

3. Conduct some personal Bible studies by applying the
    information provided in this study.

    Study #1: What God Does with Sin

    Psalm 32:1   God forgives/covers our sins.

    Psalm 32:2   God does not impute iniquity (God
                      does not hold our sins against us).

    Psalm 103:12   God removes our transgressions as far
                      as the east is from the west.

    Isaiah 1:18   Our sins are changed from scarlet to as
                      white as snow.

    Isaiah 38:17   God casts our sins behind His back
                      where He "cannot" see them.

    Isaiah 43:25   God blots out our sins and remembers
                      them no more.

    Isaiah 55:7   God has mercy and abundantly pardons.

    Micah 7:19   God casts our sins into the depths of
                      the sea.

Matthew 26:28 God remits our sins/He forgives our sins.

John 1:29 God takes away the sins of the world.

Hebrews 1:3 God purges our sins/purifies us from sins.

1 John 1:9 God cleanses us from sin.

Study 2: Bible Be's

Be at peace.	Job 22:21
Be strong/courageous.	Joshua 1:6
Be perfect/spiritually mature.	Matthew 5:48
Be of good cheer.	Matthew 14:27
Be kind.	Ephesians 4:32
Be patient.	James 5:7
Be submissive/under authority.	1 Peter 5:5
Be humble.	1 Peter 5:5
Be sober/serious about God and vigilant.	1 Peter 5:8

Be diligent/spiritually aware.   Peter 3:14

Study 3: Some Sure Things

Thou shalt surely die.   Genesis 2:17

Be sure your sins will find you out.   Numbers 32:23

The foundation of God standeth   2 Timothy 2:19
sure.

The sure word of the prophecy/   2 Peter 1:19
revelation of God.

Surely I come quickly.   Revelation
22:20